TO _____

FROM _____

RETIRE & REJOICE

BLACKIE SCOTT

ILLUSTRATIONS BY BILL JOHNSON

PEACHTREE PUBLISHERS, LTD.

Published by
PEACHTREE PUBLISHERS, LTD.
494 Armour Circle, N.E.
Atlanta, Georgia 30324

Manufactured in the United States of America

10 9 8 7 6 5 4 3 2 1

Illustrations by Bill Johnson

Library of Congress Catalog Number 88-61460

ISBN 0-934601-60-7

8-copy counter display ISBN 0-934601-61-5

"The Station," from the book A PENNY'S WORTH OF MINCED HAM by
Robert Hastings, Copyright   1986 by The Board of Trustees, Southern
Illinois University. Reprinted with permission.

DEDICATED WITH LOVE TO

MY JACK

(THE MOST PATIENT RETIREE IN THE WORLD)

CONTENTS

ACKNOWLEDGMENTS

Many of the quotes, quips, and sayings are of unknown origin. Credit is given when known. If any of your relatives should receive credit for anything found here, I am sure you will let me know!

I have copied bumper stickers, pillow tops, plaques, and have even remembered a few.

My two sisters, Mary Frances and Helen, contributed two special thoughts — THE TWENTY-THIRD POUND and THE PRAYER FOR THE RETIREE. Each was "copied."

To all of your unknown authors, thank you for making my book complete.

I am grateful to the artist Bill Johnson who captured my ideas and aspirations, and expressed them so beautifully in illustrations.

"YOU BETTER BELIEVE WE'RE INDEPENDENT!"

ONE

RETIREMENT

(Let's Hang it Up)

"Retirement" is that word we've all heard since we picked up our first paycheck. Sometime, someday . . . and now, here we are, facing this unknown. Not only do we face retirement; now the world knows just how old we are! Don't despair. I have found the secret of staying young. Eat sensibly; work hard; worship regularly; and lie about your age! It is acceptable behavior to celebrate the same birthday again and again and again.

In this century, we have gained 26 years of longevity. These "bonus years" can, and should be, fulfilling and fun.

As the wife of a retiree and a friend of many, I'm sure the key to happiness is attitude. Dr. Norman Cousins has proved that laughter can actually change our physical being. Following a hearty laugh, beta endorphins are released into our bodies, promoting healing and a sense of wellbeing. Now, really, if a good "belly laugh" is equivalent to a pill, save your money!

This book is written in hopes that you will see a bit of yourself in it and laugh. Many situations were prompted by "on-hand experiences" from friends; and, I must confess, I've been a covert observer on the world of seniors.

It must be FUN TO RETIRE. But don't forget to oil the wheels on that rocking chair, for you are going places! Where? I'm sure you don't have the answer, nor do I; but it will be fun.

RELAX! ENJOY!

"NOW, WHAT ARE WE GOING TO DO WITH <u>OUR</u> DAY?"

A reward of retirement is being able to hire someone to mow the lawn while you play golf FOR EXERCISE!

*

You're retired when you don't care where your wife goes just as long as you don't have to go along.

*

If you are too busy to be miserable, you will be happy.

*

Retiree, musing over his forty-year watch: "I wonder why a gold watch *now* when time is suddenly so unimportant!"

*

Overheard in a retirement village: "Before I die, I'm going to sell our talking parrot to the neighborhood gossip."

*

One retiree was the eternal optimist. He was always in a good mood, sitting on GO for any activity. "Worry over the future" was not even in his vocabulary. Asked his secret, he replied: "Live today. I don't even buy green bananas!"

"NOW, MILDRED, RELAX! REMEMBER, WE'RE RETIRED!"

"DARLING, I SAID GIVE A HINT OF YOUR FIGURE, NOT A DETAILED BLUEPRINT!"

TWO

ADJUSTMENTS

(Don't Call the Chiropractor)

You reach a point in life when, although you have not officially joined the retirement ranks, you have many in your circle of friends who have. You become aware through these friends that retirement cannot be taken for granted.

There are adjustments, surprises, and many rewards. I have daily reminders of these experiences. They are shared, usually secretly, by the retired couple.

Mildred called yesterday: "You remember how often I've tried to get George to put a little color on his hair? He would have no part of it. Well, now that our young neighbor, who's always sunning on her patio, has moved in, what do I hear this morning from 'ole' George? 'What was the name of that comb-on stuff for my hair?'"

Later in the week, I ran into George; and he was curious about the cost of night creams. He had checked the department store statement. Mildred's cream, "Hold Back the Years," was $48 an ounce!!

Let's face it, we're in this together!! A sense of humor and respect for each other will carry us through these years.

It's not the years that make us grow, but the changes; and it's the changes, not the years, that matter.

I'm amazed at the number of persons starting a second career after retirement and the scores who never retire.

To quote:

* Barbara Cartland, 86-year-old writer, "I think old people are so much better when they have something to do. Nobody yet has ever been known to die from overwork." (1)

* Alice Faye, 72-year-old former movie queen, "It's been 25 years since I made my last film, but the old rocking chair hasn't got me yet." (2)

* The **great** George Burns, 92 years old, ". . . fall in love with what you're doing for a living." (3) He did; and we've stayed in love with him. You really do send out a special energy to all ages as you face life with a smile.

* Art Linkletter, TV personality, author, humorist, lecturer, 75 years old, says, "It takes guts to grow old." (4)

I've read that Bette Davis has a pillow in her house with the words "Old Age is not for Sissies."

Bumper Sticker: AVENGE YOURSELF. LIVE LONG ENOUGH
                    TO BE A PROBLEM TO YOUR CHILDREN.

*

Age is a matter of mind. If you don't mind, it doesn't matter.

*

Just-retired husband standing in middle of bathroom with a large packing box from the office, filled with multivitamins, antacids, tranquilizers, etc. He calls to wife, "Honey, how about moving your stuff to the guest bathroom?"

*

Mildred had always been the grocery shopper and enjoyed her trips to the market, usually discovering something new. After George retired, he selected grocery shopping as his task and **took over**. Mildred stopped by the market one day and was heard speaking into the fruit bins: "I've missed you, but he says he shops more efficiently."

*

Scene on trash pickup day two weeks before Christmas:

Beside the neatly packaged trash on the curbing was an old, well-worn, comfortable chair with a very rotund man occupying same. His wife was at the front door calling to him: "Come on in, George. Your new one comes today. You're embarrassing me."

FOR SOME REASON, I FEEL IT'S NOT THE MODEST
ANNIVERSARY GIFT THE CHILDREN HAVE IN MIND."

Wife, with calculator in hand, berating recently-retired husband: "You know you still have 47 days of sick leave coming. Why won't they pay us for these?"

*

Wife to husband: "Twin beds or separate, what's the difference?" Husband's terse comeback: "Simple. Living alone or living with me."

*

I heard someone say, "Growing older is a journey from passion to compassion."

*

Overheard following a presentation to a group of seniors — this senior has all the answers: Rule #1 — **Never** lay your wallet or your glasses down, anywhere, anytime!!

*

A former avid bird watcher remarked sweetly, "So, I don't see the birds as well; I'll enjoy the trees."

*

Following a very lavish celebration at a retirement dinner, the guest of honor made this remark: "I'm not retiring out of a job. I'm retiring **into** life."

"HE'S SUDDENLY DECIDED YOU'RE **NOT** TOO EXPENSIVE!"

The gift industry is enjoying the seniors with delightful products. My favorites are these three decorative pillow tops:

> Youth is a gift of nature
> Middle age is a work of art.
>
> I'm somewhere between the **Blue Lagoon**
> And **On Golden Pond.**
>
> Age and treachery
> Will overcome youth and skill.

After cajoling her husband for 40 years to go to church, she finally gave up. Recently, she noticed his dialogue was different. "I'm going fishing, God willing." This new phrase was automatically added at every opportunity. She candidly asked: "Why are you suddenly adding 'God willing?'" His sly response was: "Well, just in case you're right, I thought it's about time I make a few points."

THREE

ATTITUDE

(*Trust Me, Have I Ever Been Wrong?*)

The key to successful retirement is A.A. No, not what you're thinking! Activity and Attitude!!

Don't let this be said of you: "Your mind is like concrete — thoroughly mixed and permanently set!!"

*

Husband standing on porch, wife en route from mailbox reading a letter. She: "The Joneses are going to stop on their way to Disney." He: "I will not have them even for one night. Their Christmas letters have made me sick for 40 years."

*

I was riding with a friend and noticed she had taped a radio station in place. She had loaned her car to her grandson. When it was returned, she turned the key — Rock and Roll blasted! She broke her sculptured nails trying to find her golden-oldie station. Now, it's permanently in place.

Don't put up your umbrella until it **really** rains!

*

It takes the combination — rain and sunshine — to make a rainbow.

*

Better to remain silent and be thought a fool than to speak and remove all doubt.

— Abraham Lincoln

*

A pipe gives a wise man time to think and a fool something to stick in his mouth!

*

Sometimes it takes a lot of thought . . . and effort . . . and **downright determination** to be agreeable.

*

By swallowing evil words unsaid, no one has ever yet harmed his stomach.

— Winston Churchill

*

Nothing is really work unless you would rather be doing something else.

"WHAT DO YOU MEAN—NO REASON TO SHAVE?"

Leisure is a beautiful garment, but it will not do for constant wear.

*

Those who **think** they know it all are very annoying to those of us who **do**.

*

To fill the hour, that is happiness.

> — Ralph Waldo Emerson
> "Experience"

*

Wife on phone, obviously enjoying her eleventh extended conversation of the day. Husband, shaking head, says, "and to think — I was a time management specialist."

*

Don't take life too seriously — you'll never get out of it alive.

> — Bugs Bunny

*

Bumper Sticker: WHEN WE ARE OVER THE HILL, WE PICK UP SPEED.

*

This store owner really knows his customers:

Sign in large Florida convenience store: Call home now! Save a trip . . . what did you forget?

THANKSGIVING VALUES
MEAT
POULTRY
SHE ONLY DOES MICROWAVE AND LEAN CUISINE
WELL, I'VE BOUGHT A SMOKE ALARM- WHEN IT GOES OFF THE TURKEY SHOULD BE DONE

Two retirees were "cooling it" in a small town jail, following a sentence for fishing out of season.

First fisherman: "That's really a stiff sentence, and we **did** have our licenses!"

Second Fisherman: "Don't worry, we'll be out in no time. My wife hasn't let me finish a sentence in forty years!"

I KNOW IT'S THE 3RD OF THE MONTH...
BUT TODAY'S A HOLIDAY!

This thought appeared in Ann Landers' column in NEWSDAY in 1985. Its effect was overwhelming. All the "get around to its" were moved to the front burner. Trips were taken, relationships were healed, decisions were made.

It appeared again December 2, 1987 in THE ATLANTA JOURNAL. This bit of prose by R. J. Hastings says it all.

THE STATION

Tucked away in our subconscious minds is an idyllic vision. We see ourselves on a long, long trip that almost spans the continent. We're traveling by passenger train; and out the windows we drink in the passing scene of cars on nearby highways, of children waving at a crossing, of cattle grazing on a distant hillside, of smoke pouring from a power plant, of row upon row of corn and wheat, of flatlands and valleys, of mountains and rolling hillsides, of city skylines and village halls, of biting winter and blazing summer and cavorting spring and docile fall.

But, uppermost in our minds, is the final destination. On a certain day, at a certain hour, we will pull into the station. There will be bands playing and flags waving. And, once we get there, so many wonderful dreams will come true. So many wishes will be fulfilled, and so many pieces of our lives finally will be neatly fitted together like a completed jigsaw puzzle. How restlessly we pace the aisles, damning the minutes for loitering . . . waiting, waiting, waiting for the station.

However, sooner or later, we must realize there is no one station, no one place to arrive at once and for all. The true joy of life is the trip. The station is only a dream. It constantly outdistances us.

"When we reach the station, that will be it!" we cry. Translated, it means, "When I'm 18, that will be it. When I buy a new Mercedes-Benz 450 SL, that will be it! When I put the last kid through college, that will be it! When I have paid off the mortgage, that will be it! When I win a promotion, that will be it! When I reach the age of retirement, that will be it! I shall live happily ever after!"

Unfortunately, once we get "it," then "it" disappears. The station somehow hides itself at the end of an endless track.

"Relish the moment" is a good motto, especially when coupled with Psalm 118:24: "This is the day which the Lord hath made; we will rejoice and be glad in it." It isn't the burdens of today that drive men mad. Rather, it is regret over yesterday or fear of tomorrow. Regret and fear are twin thieves who would rob us of today.

So, stop pacing the aisles and counting the miles. Instead, climb more mountains, eat more ice cream, go barefoot oftener, swim more rivers, watch more sunsets, laugh more, and cry less. LIFE MUST BE LIVED AS WE GO ALONG. THE STATION WILL COME SOON ENOUGH.

I have learned so much since I was 70 years old; more within the last 10 years than any other decade. Why should I quit?

— Pearl Buck

*

I used to burn, but now I smoulder;
I used to boil, but now I simmer.
Is this getting older or better?

*

To me, old age is 10 years older than I am.

— Bernard Baruch

*

I'm saving that rocker for the day when I feel as old as I really am.

— Dwight D. Eisenhower

*

A man is only as old as the woman he feels.

— Groucho Marx

*

One should never trust a woman who tells her age. A woman who would tell that would tell anything.

— Oscar Wilde

*

Telling his Kentucky voters why they should elect him U. S. Senator, Alben W. Barkley said, "I'm old enough to know how and young enough to do it."

*

Middle age is when you're sitting home on Saturday night, the telephone rings, and you hope it isn't for you.

— Ogden Nash

*

I'll never make the mistake of being seventy again.

— Casey Stengle

*

I will tell you that my age varies according to the day and the people I happen to be with. When I'm bored, I feel very old; and since I'm extremely bored with you, I'm going to be 1,000 years old in five minutes if you don't get the hell out of here at once!

— Gabrielle "Coco" Chanel
to a reporter

"HE'LL BE RIGHT OVER WITH THE LADDER—
JUST WATCHING SOME SILLY BALL GAME."

FOUR

LAUGHTER

(Your "Funny Bone" Is the Key to Good Health)

Will Rogers is quoted as saying, "We are all here for a spell, get all the good laughs you can."

Humor is golden; and, if it provokes laughter, it's magic. For many of us, it is a natural reaction; to some, a learned response.

A famous lieutenant commander in the navy retired. His wife was known for her sunny personality and love of people, but her house was not "ship shape." A clean house meant a swept step as you entered, a cleared chair for you to sit in, and a clean cup for your coffee. After several months of "adjustment," her husband commented, "One of the advantages of living in an unstructured home is that we are constantly making exciting discoveries."

My dears, the lieutenant commander had to find humor; or he would have returned to the ship.

I think she must have penned this: "Dull women have immaculate houses."

The most important piece of luggage is, and will remain, a joyful heart.

*

Laughter is God's hand on the shoulder of this "ole" world.

*

If you must cry over spilled milk, at least **condense** it.

*

The classic joke teller at "The Club" had a unique style. His stories were never rambling, always brief — a short pause, then the punchline. Usually, he walked away as his friends held their sides in laughter. His reason for this style: "If I stretch it out too long, my audience has time to think of one to tell me."

*

The man who can smile when things go wrong has thought of someone to blame it on.

Laugh, and the world laughs with you. Snore, and you sleep alone!

*

A hearty laugh is a workout for our internal organs — JOGGING INSIDE!

*

A smile is a curve that can set a lot of things straight.

*

The most lost day of all is the day on which we do not laugh.

*

Money cannot buy happiness, but it buys the kind of misery we enjoy.

*

Humor is to life what shock absorbers are to an automobile.

*

You are not fully dressed 'til you put on a smile.

*

Leisure time is when your wife can't find you.

*

You know you're getting old when the candles cost more than the cake.

— Bob Hope
at one of his birthday parties.

*

If I'd known I was going to live so long, I'd have taken better care of myself.

— Eubie Blake

*

The ages of man: youth, middle age, and "you haven't changed a bit." (The latter heard at many class reunions.)

*

Go ahead and touch me; wrinkles aren't contagious.

FIVE

HEALTH

(*Is This Covered by Medicare?*)

Mark Twain once said, "I am an old man and have known a great many troubles; but most of them never happened."

Statistics prove that a large percent of our concern is health related. Today, we are more involved with nutrition and physical fitness than ever before.

Dr. Richard Hornberger (author of **MASH**) wrote of his first weeks of retirement. "I took my own advice — lost fifty pounds, cut back on my drinking, and increased my golf." We do have more control over our lives now. "Staying fit" is the new buzz word!

*

As holiday time approaches, we frequently ask family for a "want list." A recent retiree and new member of the health club requested "colored" shorts (underwear). It seems he was the only one with stark white underclothes.

*

Hanging in my kitchen and done in cross stitch by my niece, Laura Thomas:

> I like my bifocals
> My dentures fit me fine
> My hearing aid is perfect
> But, Lordy, how I miss my mind!

*

One Sunday evening, I was sitting in a yogurt parlor with my back to an older couple. The gentleman was concerned over the late hour and insisted they should "get on home." It was only 8:30 p.m. Finally, she assured him they had plenty of time. As we were leaving, I overheard the reason for the concern. "Now, Mildred, you know it takes me a full hour to get all my pills in those little compartments in my pill suitcase."

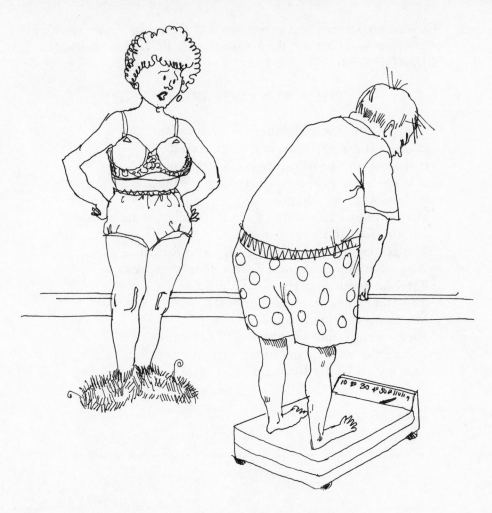

"HOW FAT CAN WE BE—AND STILL BE JOLLY?"

Wrinkles, loss of hair, loss of memory, loss of hearing — we voted —
we all agree these are not the big frustration. What is the culprit?
GAIN OF WEIGHT.

THE TWENTY-THIRD POUND

My appetite is my shepherd I always want.
It maketh me sit down and stuff myself.
It leadeth me to my refrigerator repeatedly.
It leadeth me in the path of Burger King for a Whopper.
It destroyeth my shape.
Yea, though I knoweth I gaineth, I will not stop eating
For the food tasteth so good.
The ice cream and cookies; they comfort me.
When the table is spread before me, it exciteth me
For I knoweth that I soon shall dig in.
As I filleth my plate continuously,
My clothes runneth smaller.
Surely bulges and weight shall follow me
    all the days of my life
And I shall be fat forever.

"I'D RATHER DRAG IT THAN PUSH IT!"

Two medicare patients in doctor's waiting room. With a sigh of resignation, one says: "Well, I figure from here on in, it's maintenance all the way."

*

Wife to overweight husband who continues to stay in bent-over position after having tied shoes: "What's wrong, honey? Did you lose something?" Husband: "No, it's such an effort getting down, I think I'll polish 'em, too."

*

The preoccupation with our "daily constitutional" was vividly portrayed when I observed three retired couples shopping for a week at the beach. Each had a special fruit-fiber-brand concoction for breakfast. It reminded me of an internist's comment I heard when I was very young: "He who hesitates . . . is constipated."

"OH, MY GOSH! IT'S THE TRUANT OFFICER FROM THE EXERCISE CLASS."

While dining in a posh restaurant in a resort area, an immaculately groomed older matron whispered to her husband. He didn't respond but continued to eat.

He: "Speak up, Mildred, I can't hear you."

She: "Look at me. Now, tell me, where is my filet? Six o'clock or twelve o'clock on my plate?"

He: "I'm not going to tell you. Put on your **darn** glasses."

She: "I will not. You won't wear your hearing aid!!"

*

Wife in kitchen throwing away all cleaners, soap powders, etc., as husband exclaims: "When the doctor said you should eliminate all chemicals, he didn't **mean those**."

*

My memory is the thing I forget with — a child's definition.

*

When your memory goes, forget it!

"THERE GOES THE POSTMAN WITH THE
MEDICARE SUPPLEMENT INFORMATION."

The sure sign that you have no brain is to argue with one who has none.

*

The doctor's parting comment: "Anything new in the way you feel . . . is most likely a symptom."

*

There ought to be a better way to start the day than getting up in the morning.

*

The first thing I do in the morning is breathe on the mirror and hope it fogs up.

— Early Wynn
Baseball pitcher

*

A man's health can be judged by which he takes two at a time: pills or stairs.

*

Middle age is when it is a toss up — to alter the clothes or the body.

*

DO YOU THINK THERE'LL BE ENOUGH ROOM
WHEN WE ALL BREATHE?

With the many diseases that have been discovered, my percentage is 20-1. So-o-o, I'm only 5% sick. Not bad!

*

If there's a moral to my story it's about taking care of your body. I retired at 36 years of age, and was over the hill at 33. This shouldn't happen.

— Mickey Mantle

*

If God has to give a woman wrinkles, He might at least have put them on the soles of her feet.

*

Years may wrinkle the skin, but to give up interest wrinkles the soul.

—General Douglas McArthur

In my favorite Peanuts cartoon, Snoopy appeared lying on his back, musing:

> "I can hear my heart beating,
> I can hear my stomach growling,
> I can hear my teeth grinding and my joints creaking,
> My body's so noisy, I can't sleep."

One Sunday morning, I shared the pew with a charming older couple. Each wore glasses and each had a hymnal. As we began to sing, I realized they were not going to share. He needed an extension of his arms, and she looked as though she was inspecting a diamond. I didn't know the words, so I hummed.

Have churches considered a larger print for hymnals?

"OH, I'M _SO_ SORRY. I THOUGHT YOU SAID _DAUGHTER_!"

SIX

SUDDENLY SINGLE

(Second Time 'Round)

As we move into the middle years, "second time 'round" marriages become a part of our lifestyle. The acceptable time between the termination of one relationship and the beginning of a new one has always faced the close scrutiny of family and friends. A dear minister friend made a prophetic statement:

"WOMEN GRIEVE, MEN REPLACE."

*

A woman tends to remarry because she detested her first husband. A man tends to remarry because he adored his wife...

WOMEN TRY THEIR LUCK, MEN RISK THEIRS.

It is ironic that, in second time 'round marriages, the man wants a woman with a past and the woman wants a man with a future!

*

Love's like the measles, all the worse when it comes late in life.
— Jerrold

*

Love in the autumn years and a bad cough are difficult to hide.

*

The happiness of a married man depends on the people he has not married.
— Oscar Wilde

*

When one is wise, two are happy.

*

Never marry unless you can do so into a family that will enable your children to feel proud of both sides of the house.

*

A woman without a man is like a garden without a fence.

— German proverb

*

A man is as old as he feels;
A woman is as old as she looks.

*

It is mind, not body, that makes marriages last.

*

Marry in haste — repent at leisure.

— English proverb

*

Better be an old man's darling than a young man's slave.

— English proverb

*

To be entirely happy in marriage, the same thing must be important to both.

*

A young woman married to an old man must behave like an old woman.

— Handbook of Proverbs

*

When men marry late they love their autumn child with a two-faced affection — father's and grandfather's both in one.

— O. W. Holmes

*

SEVEN

IT'S GRAND TO BE GRAND

(God's Compensation for Old Age)

My book, **It's Fun at Grandmother's House**, was the release of this great emotion that followed the birth of our first grandchild, Jamie. Five years later, we had our second, Emily Suzanne. I'm reminded of my late father's conversation. He was very proud of his three daughters and one day was complimented on his three **granddaughters**. He gave his assurance that they were his **daughters**. The older gentleman smiled and remarked, "The Lord must have smiled on you." Politely, my father inquired, "How many children do you have?" His response, "Just ten." Without any hesitation, my father remarked, "The Lord really laughed on you."

With Emily, He really did laugh on us for she is a special blessing in our lives.

Someone once said that aging has a tendency to make us "set in our ways." We don't just consciously make this decision. It happens without the usual interruptions young ones give to our lives.

Our homes are not childproof; and, for the most part, we are aware only **after** the antique bowl is broken or the priceless book has been marked with a magic marker. A few years earlier, we would have grieved; today, we are careful not to display any regret.

When we join the wonderful world of **Grandparents**, we realize for the first time what we missed in our children. I was autographing in a department store when an older gentleman handed me a copy of **It's Fun at Grandmother's House** and said, "Mrs. Scott, I was not a good father. I had to be away most of the time. I missed my children's childhood. Thank God for my second chance."

That's what they are — our second chance to love, to enjoy, to GET OUT OF OUR RUTS!

" WE DO NOT TAKE NAPS IN THE DAYTIME
UNLESS THE GRANDCHILDREN ARE HERE."

I keep a few examples of my Jamie's "art work" on my refrigerator door. I never realized how lonely a refrigerator door can be until I visited a friend with no grandchildren. Her door was filled with doctors' appointments and one square dancing reminder. I really think her children should consider that naked refrigerator door when they decide **career** not **family**.

*

Parents today are so eager to buy the perfect toy for their children. This ad caught the attention of all subscribers: **GUARANTEED TO AMUSE ANY CHILD. ABSOLUTELY SAFE. NO NEED TO WIND. NO BATTERIES REQUIRED. PORTABLE. CAN ADJUST TO ANY AREA. FOR DETAILED INFORMATION, DIAL:**

1–800–GRANDPARENTS.

"GRANDDADDY, DOES A CHAIRMAN OF THE BOARD LIKE ONE OR TWO LUMPS?"

THINGS OUR GRANDCHILDREN SAY

The most flattering comment from a grandchild was shared by a good friend:

Baby-sitting a 4-year-old can be a very physical experience. Having played with most of Whitney's active games, Grandfather suggested some quiet play. A very determined Whitney wanted to continue. After a while, he commented, "I'm sure your other Grandfather doesn't play *all* the games *all* the time." Her quick response, "I know, Grampy. You see, he doesn't play with children — he's all grown up."

*

"Why does Nana call her friends "girls" whey they really aren't?"

*

"Grandparents never say, 'We'll have to see about it later!' They do it now!"

*

"Grandma doesn't say bad words, but boy! Grandpa can say some corkers!"

"You don't have to do a good job to get a surprise — just try and you'll get it every time."

*

"Grandmothers need more hugs than mothers."

*

"My Baba told Nana he would read my story — and he went to sleep!"

*

"I hope my next tooth comes out at Grandmother's house. That tooth fairy only gives 'foldover' money."

*

"I gotta learn to fix things so I can be a good 'Pappy'."

*

"My Grandparents are not like yours. Mine are on the slow motion; you know, like on T.V."

*

"She's not old! My Granny only wears glasses to keep our baby from punching out her eyes."

*

A grandmother and grandchild were looking at some old black and white photographs. Accustomed to only color prints, the grandchild remarked, "Nana, I like the world in color. It must have been awful when everything was in black and white."

*

EIGHT

REFLECTIONS

(*It's Later than You Think*)

As the "ole" cowboy said, "We're headin' for the last roundup."

My very favorite quote is a Yiddish proverb: Old age to the unlearned is winter; to the learned, it is harvest.

*

Don't regret growing older, it is a privilege denied many.

*

Relationships with friends and family become more important. We tend to seek each other, regardless of distance, social status, or previous feelings.

*

Old and young, we are all on our last cruise. If there is a fill of tobacco among the crew, for God's sake pass it 'round; and let's have a pipe before we go.

— Robert L. Stevenson

God gave us memories so that we might have roses in December.

— J. M. Barrie

*

To be seventy years young is something far more cheerful and hopeful than to be forty years old.

— Oliver Wendell Homes

*

A great memory is fine, but the ability to forgive and forget is the test of greatness.

*

That the birds of worry can fly above your head, this you cannot change; but that they should build nests in your hair, this you can prevent!

*

A miser and a fat pig will only be of use when dead.

— Logau

The above quotation found framed and in a lawyer's office really confused me. His secretary's quiet explanation: He specializes in wills!

Never ask people to guess your age. It can force them to give an insult or to tell a loving lie.

*

A man is getting older when he:

. . . is warned to slow down by a doctor instead of a policeman.
. . . wants to see how long his car will last instead of how fast it will go.

*

On a plaque in Berta's kitchen: "I am not afraid of tomorrow, for I have seen yesterday, and I love today."

*

Old age isn't so bad when you consider the alternative.
— Maurice Chevalier

*

People who live long, who will drink the cup of life to the very bottom, must expect to meet some of the dregs.
— Benjamin Franklin

*

I hope I can recall part of a quote by a great lady of our time. Now, I am in my eighties and I have known the joy and sorrows of a full life . . . I prefer to remember the good times.

— Rose Fitzgerald Kennedy

*

Old wood is the best to burn,
Old wine to drink,
Old friends to trust,
Old authors to read.

*

Youth is for learning
Middle age for doing
Old age is for enjoying.

*

Age matters only when one is aging. Now that I have arrived at a **great** age, I might just as well be twenty.

— Picasso

*

Man to cemetery salesman in a cemetery garden:

"If I wait 'til Wednesday, will I get an extra senior citizen's discount?"

*

Wife, reading husband's will, asks:

"Are you **sure** you want your funeral at 2:00 a.m.?"

He: "I'm sure. Then you'll find out just how many friends we **really** have."

*

Never put off 'til tomorrow what you can avoid altogether.

*

May your igloo be warm
May your lattern have oil
May you find that peace for your heart.
— Eskimo Proverb

*

PRAYER FOR THE RETIREE

Lord, thou knowest better than I would know myself that I am growing older and that someday I shall be old. Keep me from the fatal habit of thinking I must expound on every subject and on every occasion. Release me from craving to straighten out everybody's affairs. Make me thoughtful but not moody, helpful but not bossy. With my vast store of wisdom, it seems a pity not to use it all; but thou knowest, Lord, that I want a few friends at the end.

Keep my mind free from recital of endless details, give me wings to get to the point. Seal my lips on my aches and pains. They are increasing, and love of rehearsing them is becoming sweeter as the years go by. I dare not ask for grace to enjoy the tales of others' pains, but help me to endure with patience.

I dare not ask for improved memory but for growing humility and a lessening of cocksureness when my memory seems to clash with the memory of others. Teach me the glorious lesson that, occasionally, I could be mistaken. Keep me reasonably sweet — I do not want to be a saint — some of them are so hard to live with; but a sour old person is one of the crowning works of the devil.

Give me the ability to find unexpected talents in people and to see good things in unexpected places. And give me, Lord, the grace to say so.

After reading this bit of prose I changed my salutation from "How are you?" to, "So good to see you, isn't it a wonderful day?". Everyday is a wonderful day, so enjoy!

FOOTNOTES

(1) Barbara Cartland, *The Atlanta Journal — The Atlanta Constitution*.

(2) Alice Faye, *50 Plus*, January 1988.

(3) George Burns, Newsmakers, *The Atlanta Journal — The Atlanta Constitution*.

(4) Art Linkletter, *The Atlanta Journal — The Atlanta Constitution*.

Blackie Scott is a native of Virginia. Trained as a registered nurse, Blackie worked in the medical profession until 1963. As a humorous speaker, Blackie speaks on various subjects including "Retire and Rejoice." Since then, Blackie has been active on the national speaking circuit. Her husband, Jack, manages Scott Enterprises. The Scotts have one daughter, Suzanne, and two granddaughters, Jamie and Emily.

Blackie is the author of two previous books. IT'S FUN TO ENTERTAIN and IT'S FUN AT GRANDMOTHER'S HOUSE. She resides in Atlanta.

Bill Johnson is a native Floridian but has lived and worked in Atlanta for the past 35 years. Besides enjoying a reputation as an established graphic designer and illustrator, he has painted and exhibited extensively and is best known for his vibrant water colors. He has taught art at Georgia State University and at the Atlanta College of Art.

Bill Johnson